VALLEY WALKS IN

Paul Buttle

Published by

ama̅ðorn

First published May, 1993
Reprinted May, 1994, March, 1996

ISBN 0 9513717 7 0
© P. Buttle 1993.
Published by Amadorn, 18 Brewery Lane, Keswick, Cumbria.
Typeset by The Keswick Studio, Keswick.
Imageset by McKane Printers, Keswick.
Printed by The Nuffield Press, Oxford.

CONTENTS

INTRODUCTION

This guide is intended mainly for people who are averse to tackling steep gradients on their walks, which is not the type of walk the Lake District is particularly well designed for, but such walks are possible and this guide covers a good many of them. The walks are actually a compilation of walks taken from two other guides I have produced in the past and a two more which are in preparation.

The walks cover a wide area of the Lake District and anyone doing all of them will obtain a good appreciation of the Lake District's rich variety of scenery. Every valley in the Lake District always seems to me to be perfect and yet each one has its own distinct quality. So there is much to discover on these walks especially if the Lake District is entirely new to you.

Are the views on valley walks as good as the views one obtains on the higher fells? Whenever I look through a collection of photographs of the Lake District I am always struck by the impressiveness of those photographs taken from the valleys. Of course this may simply reflect the fact that valley photographs are a lot easier to obtain than those shots taken from the high fells, but even when the compiler of such a collection has obviously had a wide selection of photographs to chose from it is still surprising how again and again it is the valley shot one notices most. The critic and writer John Ruskin who lived in the Lake District disdained of the idea of climbing fells. For him the fells could be appreciated best from the valleys and climbing them was to be avoided. All that said you will notice it is a fell view that adorns the cover of this guide.

Order of Walks

The walks have been ordered firstly according to the distance involved and then secondly according to the height of ascent involved. So the shortest walk appears first and the longest last. This roughly reflects also the amount of effort required to do each walk as well, though if it was to reflex it accurately then the Duddon Valley and the Borrowdale walks would have a higher placing in view of the amount of climbing involved in them.

Heights of Ascent

Though this guide, as I have said, is intended mainly for people who are averse to making ascents no walk can avoid some degree of climbing, unless it be in Holland. However in this guide only on those walks where the total feet of ascent is above a thousand will most walkers have any sense of climbing. Those walks are the Borrowdale, the Two Langdales, and the Duddon Valley walks. The average gradient of the 'steepest' of these walks, the Duddon Valley walk, is less than 1 in 30. (Or as our new continentally inspired roadsigns would have it 3%, but 3% of what? Vertical?)

Suggested Times of Walks

Where these are made they are just that, suggested, based on the false assumption that you will not stop nor tarry for an instant, because it is almost certain that you will. They are meant simply to be a rough guide. If you want to you can no doubt do them in a quicker time than the time suggested, if on the other hand you want to do the walks leisurely you should add another hour, or even two, to each walk.

Choice of Map

The Ordnance Survey 'One Inch' Tourist map is the best map to use with this guide as it covers all the walks described in this guide. Though a relatively large map, at a scale of 1:63,630, it should be more than suffecent given the directional notes in this guide. It only has one fault, a quite unforgivable flaw: some years ago the Ordnance Survey diligently and meticulously metricated all the height measurements on it, thus causing me, and I am sure thousands of others, hours of mental computing to work out what these heights are in feet. (You will gather I am in no way enamoured with continental ways of measuring things.)

Public Transport

Public transport in the Lake District is always changing, usually for the worse. At the time of writing all but two or three of the starting points of the walks in this guide are served by some form of public transport including miniature steam trains and postbuses. Fortunately the county of Cumbria has a good travel information service called 'Travel Link' provided by Cumbria County Council. Any enquiries concerning public transport is best made to them. Their number is Carlise (01228) 812 812.

Closing Gates

Valley walking inevitably involves crossing stiles and passing through gates. When you pass through a gate always make sure to close it behind you.

Caithir siúl sa gleannta is doimhne chun
thaithiniúint a thabhairt do na h-ardúin is aoirde

de réir Theodore Roosevelt

THE BUTTERMERE CIRCUIT

Distance	4 1/2 miles
Total feet of Ascent	200 feet
Suggested Time	2 hours
Starting Point	Buttermere village car park (NY 174 169)

This walk is probably the most attractive level walk in the Lake District. It hardly needs any directions as it is so straightforward, apart from suggesting that the walk should be done clockwise round the lake. The reason for this is simple enough; the best views are to be had looking up the valley which can't be seen so well from the south-western shoreline of the lake as much of it is thickly wooded with conifer trees. The great majority of people who do walk around the lake however tend to do so anti-clockwise, so be prepared to receive several salutations.

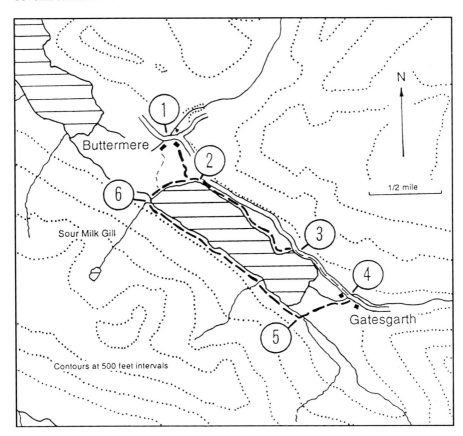

1   Beginning from the Bridge Hotel turn right to follow the main road for fifty yards and turn right into the farmyard of Syke Farm which is signposted as being a bridleway leading to the lakeshore. The path begins from the end of the farmyard and leads to the northern corner of the lake. (1/2 mile)

2   The path is so distinct there is no problem following it hereon. Where however it links back to the B5289, as you will probably notice, there is a a permissive path which continues a little further along the lakeshore before itself linking up with the B5289. (1 1/4 miles)

3   Unfortunately it is now necessary to continue along the roadway as far as Gatesgarth farm where, immediately after crossing the bridge crossing Gatesgarthdale Beck, next to a post box, is the start of an indicated bridleway back to Buttermere initially following the side of Gatesgarthdale Beck.(1/4 mile)

4   Within a hundred yards the path links onto a trackway leading from the farmyard which almost immediately splits in two. Follow the right-hand branch which leads to a wooden bridge crossing Warnscale Beck across which is a five bar gate and kissing gate. (1/2 mile)

5   Passing through the gate turn immediately right onto a signposted public bridleway leading back to Butteremere village. Entering a conifer wood the path splits in two but within a few hundred yards the two paths merge back together. Reaching the western corner of the lake the path crosses the foot of Sour Milk Gill and then swings round to the right to a footbridge crossing the lake's outflow. (1 1/2 miles)

6   From the bridge a distinct track leads back to Buttermere village, but by turning right it is possible to continue along a permissive path which follows the northern shore of the lake and links back onto the path you started on. (3/4 mile)

MARTINDALE

Distance	4 1/2 miles
Total Feet of Ascent	400 feet
Suggested Time	2 hours
Starting Point	St Martins Old Church (NY 434 184)
Car Parking	In front of church.
Public Transport	Ulswater Motoryacht Glenridding to Howtown Pier. Seasonal only Tel. 07684 82229

To some extent Martindale is cut off from the rest of the Lake District, most motorists seem to deem it too much out of the way to bother with. This then has the pleasing effect of making Martindale a relatively quiet valley, and yet once there it is unlikely you will be able to conceive of there being a more appealing dale anywhere else. Martindale, the name of which apparently derives from an ancient cross dedicated to St Martin which once stood in the valley, is actually not one single valley but two, Boardale and Bannerdale, or three if you include Rampsgill. They are so close to each other however, and each seems so like an extension of the other it is hard not to think of them as one single valley.

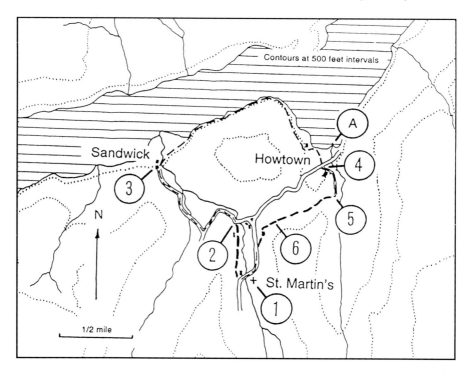

A   (If begining the walk from Howtown Pier walk directly from the pier to the roadway and turn right. A few hundred yards along the roadway turn first left, and from here follow note 4 onwards.)

1   From the church follow the road south across a stone bridge. A hundred yards or so after crossing the bridge on your right is the start of a bridleway leading behind Winter Crag farm. After passing a very attractive little cottage the bridleway comes to a surfaced road. (1/2 mile)

2   Here turn left and follow the road. Where it comes to a junction turn right and follow the road to Sandwick. (1 mile)

3   At the end of the road a trackway continues to the right over a broad wooden bridge. This leads without difficulty round the base of Hallin Fell along the shoreline of Ullswater back to Howtown bay. A hundred yards after passing behind a large cream coloured house, Waternook, the path comes to a kissing gate. Here turn left through the kissing gate and down a flight of steps on to the trackway leading to Waternook. Turn right on the trackway and follow it to the Martindale road. *(1 3/4 miles) (If returning back to the Howtown pier here turn left, otherwise...)*

4   Immediately across the road is what appears to be a surfaced driveway to the Howtown Hotel. The road however leads behind the hotel and where it splits you should take the right hand branch to Cote Farm as far as the first cattle grid. (1/4 mile)

5   Here turn right and follow the stone wall to your right uphill. This soon becomes a very evident grassy trackway, a bridleway, leading over Hallin Hause. Where however this bridleway begins to dip down and turn right, where there is a water hydrant marker, continue walking straight ahead along a very indistinct path following the left hand side of the wall ahead. The path soon comes to a small six bar gate. (1/2 mile)

6   Passing through the gate the path leads to two attractive cottages called Cotehow. Below them you should observe the valley's old methodist church and beside it an old reading room. Both are now domiciles. The building opposite them is the valley's former school. The right of way leads right through the front yard of Cotehow cottages and down to the roadway, though it is possible to skirt round the wall of the yard if you feel you are intruding too much on their privacy. On reaching the road turn left and follow the road back to St Martin's church. (1/2 mile)

THE NEWLANDS VALLEY

Distance	5 miles, less if starting from Gutherscale.
Total feet of Ascent	500 feet
Suggested Time	2 1/2 hours
Starting Point	A Hawes End Pier, 1 1/2 mile SW of Keswick (NY 250 213) or
	B Gutherscale Car Park (NY 247 212)

This is a walk through a very peaceful pastoral valley surrounded by many graceful hills. Although the outward route is close to the return route, and even the same in some sections, they are suprisingly different from each other. Be sure to visit the valley's church on the walk's return section. Its tiny adjacent former schoolroom is especially interesting.

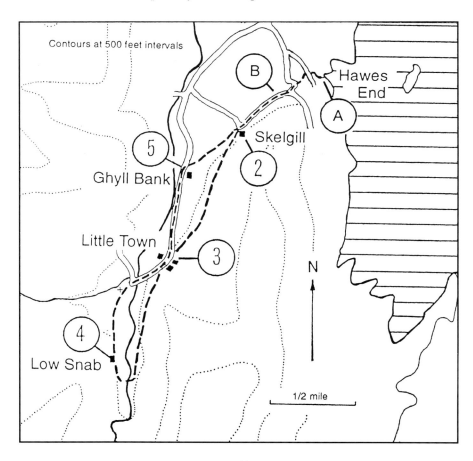

A   Beginning from Hawes End Pier, which is possible to reach from Keswick by public launch, enquire at Keswick's Moot Hall Information Centre for further information, turn right and walk uphill along a broad pathway across an access road and a few yards further on to a public road. Follow the road uphill across a cattle grid to a sharp hairpin bend where there is also a road junction. Here bear right and follow the road to Skelgill Farm. (1/2 mile)

B   Beginning from Gutherscale Car Park on the side of Cat Bells turn left and follow the road south to Skelgill Farm. (1/4 mile)

2   At Skelgill Farm the road turns sharp right and leads downhill. Follow the road's descent a few yards, but after passing an old water trough turn left off the road onto a path leading immediately past the gable end of the farm. This path leads to Little Town, across a series of fields mostly following a line of hawthorn bushes. (1 mile)

3   On joining the road at Little Town turn left and walk through the hamlet. Immediately after passing the hamlet's last house follow an obvious trackway veering off to the left to the head of the valley. Follow this trackway to a point where the wall, which the trackway comes to follow, turns right away from the track towards Low Snab Farm. At this point continue along the path which follows the wall across Newlands Beck to Low Snab Farm. *(Pots of tea and other refreshments are usually available at the farm in the summer.)* (1 mile)

4   From the farm follow the farm's access road past Newlands Church to a gated road junction. Here turn right and walk uphill through Little Town and along the road for another half mile to Ghyll Bank Farm. (1 1/4 miles)

5   A few yards past Ghyll Bank on your right locate a small gate from which a signposted path leads back to Skelgill Farm. From Skelgill Farm retrace your route back to your starting point. (3/4 or 1 mile)

THE RUSLAND VALLEY

Distance	5 miles
Total feet of Ascent	400 feet
Suggested time	2 hours
Starting point	Oxen Park, 7 miles south of Coniston (SD 318 873)
Car Parking	Outside village hall, on the road to Lowick

A countryside ramble over a quiet secluded landscape with a surprisingly varied terrain of heath land, woodland, marshland as well as farmland with prospects of wooded hills all around. There is a public house in the middle of Oxen Park village.

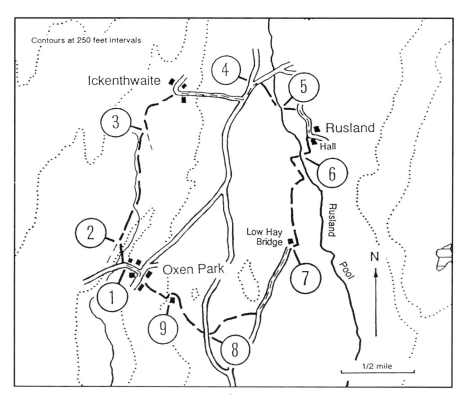

1   A few yards along the road from the village hall, in the direction of Lowick, is a trackway leading off to the right signposted as leading to Stock Farm. Within two hundred yards the track branches in two. Follow the left-hand branch which fords a stream. Within another few hundred yards this joins another trackway. (1/4 mile)

2   Here turn right and follow the trackway northwards to Ickenthwaite. The route soon becomes a confusion of trackways but fortunately the bridleway you should be following, which soon becomes a rough pathway, is well way-marked with a series of arrows. Eventually it joins another trackway. (3/4 mile)

3   Here turn left. The track eventually reaches a narrow roadway at the hamlet of Ickenthwaite. Here turn right. The road descends downhill and eventually reaches a road junction. Here turn left and then take the first turn right on to the Rusland Hall road. (1 mile)

4   Within a hundred yards along this road a trackway leads off to the right. Some two hundred yards along this trackway, just before reaching the river Rusland Pool, is a kissing gate next to a six bar gate on the right-hand side of the track. Pass through the kissing gate and turn left to follow the left-hand side of the field you enter to another kissing gate which gives access to a foot-bridge crossing Rusland Pool. (1/4 mile)

5   On the other side of the river is the terminus of a trackway. Here turn right and follow the trackway to a roadway. Here turn right and follow the road to the gate house of Rusland Hall. Here bear right again on to a trackway lead-ing round the back of Rusland Hall and signposted as being a public footpath leading to Bouth and Oxen Park. This leads to a bridge spanning Rusland Pool. (1/2 mile)

6   On the other side of the bridge is a signposted footpath leading off to the left which follows a series of waymark posts. About a quarter of a mile from the bridge the path appears to branch in two. Bear right following a series of white posts leading through some woodland. The path finally emerges from the wood by way of a foot bridge leading to a house called Low Hay Bridge. (1/2 mile)

7   Follow the narrow surfaced road leading uphill from the house, signposted as being a footpath leading to Bouth. A few hundred yards after crossing a cattlegrid a lone signpost indicates a footpath leading uphill to the right. There is little or no evidence of a path but fortunately the right of way is waymarked with a series of waymark posts which lead to a metal gate, through which it then follows the wall to your left, through two more gates, to a roadway. (1 mile)

8   Here turn right. Fifty yards along the road is a signpost indicating a public footpath leading off to the left to a six bar gate. From the gate the right of way heads directly towards the farm you see ahead of you, by way of two more gates. Passing the right-hand side of the farm complex the right of way comes to the farm's driveway. (1/2 mile)

9   Turn left. Walk fifteen yards into the farmyard and turn right through a metal gate and follow the left-hand side of the field you enter to another metal gate. Pass through this gate and follow the wall to your right back to Oxen Park village. (1/4 mile)

ST. JOHN'S IN THE VALE

Distance	5 1/2 miles
Total feet of Ascent	500 feet
Suggested Time	2 hours
Starting Point	St John's in the Vale Church (NY 306 225)
	2 1/2 miles S.E. of Keswick
Car Parking	In front of church

This circular walk takes in two valleys; St. John's in the Vale and the Naddle valley. St. John's in the Vale is a very attractive, peaceful valley yet it receives surprisingly little attention. The Naddle valley also has a lot of rustic appeal though it is unfortunately marred by the sound of traffic rushing along the A591. The walk starts from the little church which serves both these valleys situated on the lowest point of the High Rigg and Low Rigg ridge which separates them. It is best to approach the church from the B5322 which runs through St. John's in the Vale.

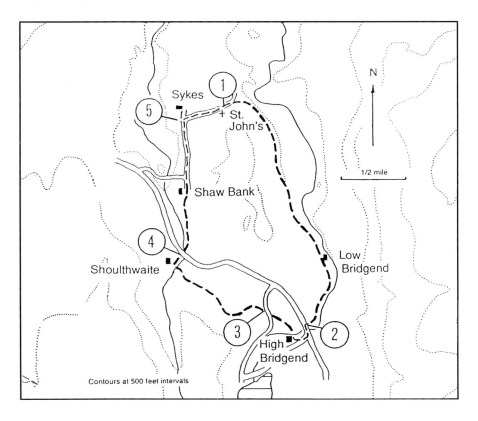

1   From the church walk downhill along the road a few hundred yards east-wards and branch off the road through the first gate on your right onto an indicated bridleway. A mile from the church, just before reaching a small barn, the bridleway appears to branch in two, the left branch leading across the valley to a stone bridge. Here take the righthand branch, it is in fact a footpath, which leads behind the barn and on to Low Bridgend Farm and eventually to the main Keswick to Ambleside road. (2 1/4 miles)

2   Here turn left and take the first turn right to High Bridgend Farm. Pass through the farm and the farm's sheep pens down to a footbridge spanning St. John's Beck. Cross the bridge and follow a waymarked path up to a group of barns. Pass between the barns along a distinct trackway to a surfaced road. Here turn right. Within twenty yards pass through the first gate on your left onto a broad trackway. (1/2 mile)

3   Within a short distance the trackway branches in two. Take the left-hand branch. Where this trackway begins to climb uphill observe a grassier track-way leading off to the right. Follow this trackway to the outbuildings of Shoulthwaite Farm. Then follow the farm access road to the main Keswick to Ambleside road. (1 mile)

4   Cross straight over the road to a small stone stile next to a bridge. This leads to a small field across which is another stone stile giving access to a section of old road. From this second stile diagonally opposite to the right is the start of a signposted bridleway. This leads to Shaw Bank where it becomes a narrow surfaced road. Follow this road northwards ignoring the turning to the left which leads back to the main Keswick to Ambleside road. Reaching the entrance to Sykes Farm the road becomes unsurfaced and branches in two. (1 mile)

5   Here follow the righthand branch which leads back to St. John's in the Vale Church. (1/2 mile)

THE DUDDON VALLEY

Distance	6 miles
Total feet of Ascent	1000 feet
Suggested Time	3 hours
Starting Point	Seathwaite Church (SD 229 962)
Car Parking	Layby just north of church

The Duddon valley is more boulder strewn and has more rocky outcrops than any other valley in the Lake District, which makes it the wildest looking valley in Lakeland. This valley walk therefore involves some very rugged walking at times and in places is more similar to a fellwalk than an easy low level saunter. Essentially the walk is a slightly elevated traverse along both sides of the valley and therefore has some very good views. A hundred yards from the starting point is the valley pub; the Newfield Inn.

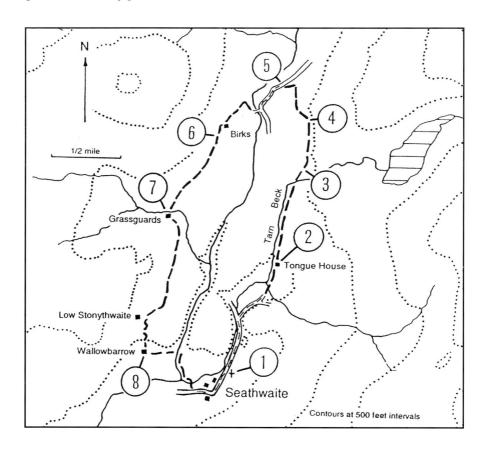

1   Walk northwards along the valley road. Just under half a mile from the church bear right on to a road signposted as leading to Coniston. Where this road branches in two bear left to reach Tongue House Farm. (1 mile)

2   Continue round the back of the farmhouse and once through a metal gate turn immediately left onto a rough trackway that takes a fairly direct line northwards to a wooden stile. From the stile onwards the right of way follows the eastern bank of Tarn Beck and a line of electricity poles. Where the course of the river veers right cross the river and continue following the line of the electricity poles towards a wall stile a few hundred yards ahead. (3/4 mile)

3   From the stile continue forward through a currently gateless gap in the next wall ahead and once through bear right to follow the side of the wall you have just passed through. Where the wall begins to contour the fellside you should be able to locate a path which gradually veers away from the wall to the boundary line of a conifer wood. (1/2 mile)

4   Follow the boundary of the wood downhill until you reach a stile crossing a wire fence. Once over the stile turn left. A yellow arrow waymark soon indicates a path which leads into the wood and then pulls uphill over a small ridge, paralell to a ruined wall. On the descent side of the ridge the path veers right from the wall and eventually reaches a forestry track. Here turn left. The track soon joins the valley road. (1/4 mile)

5   Here turn left again. A quarter of a mile along the road bear right across a narrow stone bridge, Birks Bridge, (not to be confused with the forestry bridge a few hundred yards further upstream) onto a bridleway which veers slightly right to begin with and then swings left to Birks Farm. Follow the farm's access road uphill but once over a cattle grid turn immediately left onto a trackway. This soon links with a forestry road. (3/4 mile)

6   Here turn left. Follow the forestry road a hundred yards or so uphill and then veer right on to a rough trackway. After running roughly paralell to the forestry road the trackway cuts across it, the junction is slightly staggered, dips downhill a little and then takes a level course to Grassguards Farm, the final few hundred yards having been integrated into another forestry road. (3/4 mile)

7   Follow the trackway running directly in front of the farm which eventually leads to Low Stonythwaite. A hundred yards before reaching the farm however a path leads off to the left taking a steep zigzagged course downhill to Wallowbarrow farm. (1 1/4 mile)

8   From the farm bear left out of the farmyard onto a path signposted as leading to Seathwaite and waymarked with a series of yellow arrows. This leads to a stone bridge crossing the river Duddon. Once over the bridge bear right onto a path following the river downstream. This soon veers left to cross a concrete bridge spanning a tributary of the Duddon in order to reach the main valley road. Here turn left to return back to Seathwaite. (3/4 mile)

ESKDALE

Distance	6 1/2 miles
Total feet of Ascent	Negligible
Suggested Time	2 1/2 hours
Starting Point	Boot (NY 177 010)
Car Parking	At the Burnmoor Inn with landlord's permission.

Eskdale is a wonderful valley of snug farmsteads and small deciduous woods bounded by rugged fells. The rock in the valley has a slightly pinkish colour which give the houses and even the field boundary walls a 'warm' look. The walk essentially follows the course of the river Esk, after which the valley is named, upstream to the foot of Hardknott Pass and then returns by way of the valley's main road. This is a pleasant lane to walk along when free of traffic which unfortunately is not its usual condition in high summer.

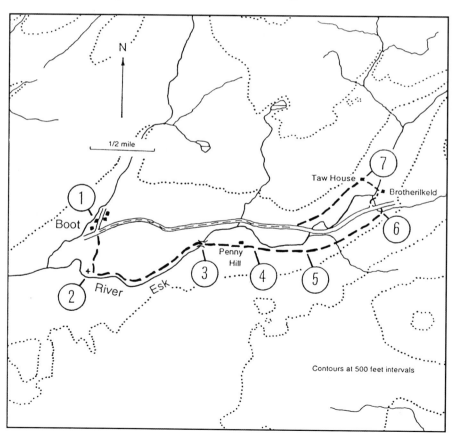

1   From the Burnmoor Inn walk back to the main valley road. Walk straight across the road onto a lane signposted as leading to the valley church. The lane leads to the River Esk on the banks of which the church is situated. (1/2 mile)

2   Here turn left and follow the pathway leading initially along the river bank. This is a distinct path which more or less paralells the river Esk until it reaches a stone bridge spanning the river. (1 mile)

3   Cross over the bridge and follow the farm access road that leads directly from it to Penny Hill Farm. A right of way, a bridleway, continues past the farm and is waymarked with a series of blue arrows that indicate it follows a rough trackway. About two hundred yards from the farm the trackway branches in two. (1/2 mile)

4   Bear left, still following the blue arrow waymarks. Passing through a gateway the trackway becomes little more than a line of ruts until it follows the outer side of a field boundary wall. Soon after crossing a small beck the bridleway reaches a sign post at the edge of a wood. (1/2 mile)

5   Here continue forward along a path the signpost indicates as leading to Hardknott, along the outer edge of the wood's boundary wall then on to a footbridge crossing the next beck, a hundred yards ahead, and then through a gateway, but NOT over the stile immediately to the left of the gate. The path continues through some woodland and then along the foot of some open fell and evenutally joins an old bridleway, which passing through two kissing gates and over a stone footbridge joins the Hardknott Pass road. (3/4 mile)

6   Here turn left. Just over a hundred yards along the road turn right on to the farm access road to Brotherilkeld farm. Just before entering the farmyard bear left onto a footpath which follows the bank of the river Esk. This soon leads to a footbridge spanning the Esk. From the other side of the bridge an enclosed path leads to Taw House Farm. (1/2 mile)

7   From Taw House Farm follow the farm access road left out of the farmyard back to the main valley road. On reaching the road turn right and follow the road back to Boot. (2 1/2 miles)

PATTERDALE

Distance	6 1/2 miles
Total Feet of Ascent	Negligible
Suggested Time	2 1/2 hours
Starting Point	Patterdale Village car park (NY 396 159)

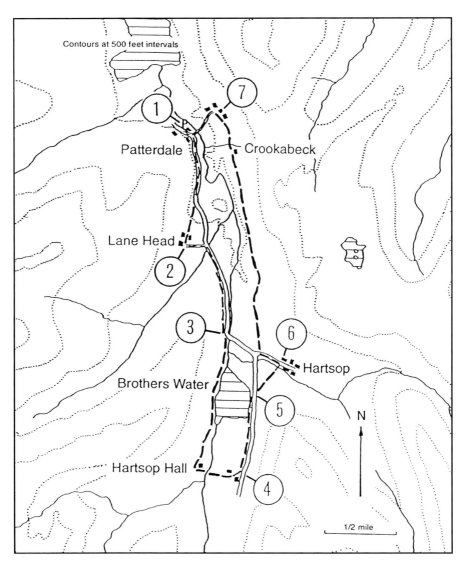

In the Patterdale area the only true level walk possible is the one described here, an elongated circuit of the valley floor itself. Unfortunately nearly half of the walk is along the side of, or little distance from, the A592, the main road which runs through the valley, which obviously detracts from the walk's tranquillity, though surprisingly not to the extent one might think.

1   From the car park turn left and follow the road south. Roughly three quarters of a mile from Patterdale Post Office a driveway veers off to the right across a cattle grid signposted as being a public footpath to Deepdale leading initially to a little hamlet called Lane Head. (1 mile)

2   At Lane Head the driveway splits in two. Follow the left hand branch which turns left and leads back to the road. On reaching the road turn right. There is now no surfaced path along the side of the road, but along the right hand side of the road is a wide grass verge across which has worn a footpath. Follow this path. Within a quarter of a mile, starting from a single birch tree, the path rises above the level of the road and leads onto a permitted path that follows the road at a slightly higher level, through National Trust land, eventually reaching the start of a trackway leading from a sharp bend in an old section of the main road. (1 mile)

3   Here turn right and follow the trackway south past the western shoreline of Brotherswater. Eventually the path comes to curve left round Hartsop Hall where it branches in two. Follow the left hand branch which soon curves right and leads across a large campsite. Leaving the campsite the trackway branches in two once more. Follow the left hand branch. Five yards before it reaches the road leading off to the left is the start of a permitted path to Brotherswater. (1 1/4 miles)

4   Follow the permitted path which parallels the main road northwards mostly at a slightly lower level. It joins the the road briefly and then drops down to follow the eastern shoreline of Brotherswater. (In wet weather this path is prone to flooding). After passing through a kissing gate the path then leads up to a second kissing gate set in the wall bordering the road.(1/2 mile)

5   Directly across the road is a five bar gate. Cross over the road and pass through the gate. This leads on to an enclosed trackway that leads to a narrow footbridge crossing Pasture Beck giving access to the small village of Hartsop. (1/4 mile)

6   On reaching the road running through the village turn left. (Though before you do so it is worth turning right to view what is one of the most appealing villages in the Lake District). Just before reaching the main road, to your right, leading north by the side of the Langton Adventure Centre, is a surfaced driveway. Continue along this driveway but where it curves right into 'Hartsop Fold' continue straight ahead along the unsurfaced trackway ahead of you. This is a delightful rustic trackway back to Patterdale village, though where it passes by an attractive dwelling called Crookabeck it may seem as if there is no longer a right of way along it, and indeed a permitted path is indicated as running behind the house; however a right of way does continue along the trackway. Within a short distance from Crookabeck it reaches a small hamlet. (2 miles)

7   Here the track joins a surfaced driveway. Turn left and follow the driveway back to the start of the walk. (1/4 mile)

THE LOWESWATER CIRCUIT

Distance	7 miles
Total feet of Ascent	400 feet
Suggested Time	2 1/2 hours
Starting Point	Scale Bridge car park (NY 149 214)

The area immediately around Loweswater lake is very gentle and pastoral yet it is also set in the midst of some very rugged and imposing mountain scenery. Indeed the view looking down the length of Crummock Water into the depth of the Buttermere valley and on to Great Gable, which is perhaps seen to its best advantage along the first mile of the walk, is one of the most impressive views in the Lake District. There are also two points on the walk where it is possible to enjoy a very civilised break for refreshments.

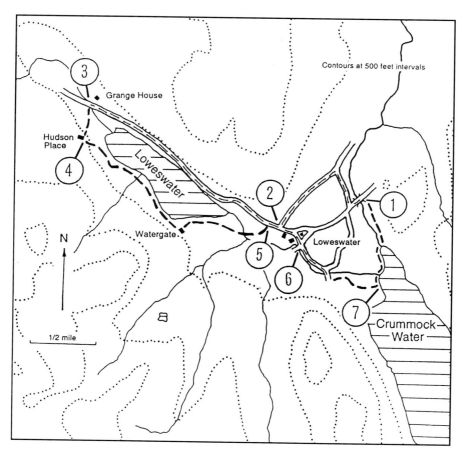

1   From the car park turn left across Scalehill Bridge and take the first turn right onto a road signposted as leading to Thackthwaite. The road soon comes to a junction. Here turn left. Within three quarters of a mile this road also comes to a road junction. (1 1/4 miles)

2   Here turn right. The road soon comes to follow the north-eastern lakeshore of Loweswater. For a few hundred yards along the lakeshore is an alternative lakeshore path one can use, but it runs through such a thick growth of bushes and saplings there is little advantage in using it. Eventually the road comes to The Grange Country House Hotel. (1 3/4 miles)

(The Grange Country House Hotel serves bar meals and teas. Its spacious lawn, where one can sit, has a marvellous quintessential Lakeland view of unbelievable beauty and yet the hotel itself lies just outside the national park.)

3   Immediately opposite the driveway of the Grange Country House Hotel is the start of a driveway leading to Hudson Place Farm also signposted as being a bridleway to Holme Wood and Fangs Brow. Follow the driveway. As it curves right into the farmyard of Hudson Place a trackway veers off to the left with a slate sign indicating it is a footpath. (1/4 mile)

4   It is in fact a bridleway and for much of its length is also a broad motorable trackway which parallels or follows the south-west shoreline of Loweswater and then passes through Watergate Farm, from where it leads back up to the Loweswater to Mockerkin road, becoming itself in its final few hundred yards a surfaced road. (1 3/4 miles)

5   On reaching the Loweswater to Mockerkin road turn right. A few hundred yards down the road take the first turn right. Where this road curves left round Loweswater church branch right, past the Kirkstile Inn, onto the road with a sign indicating that it is 'No Road to the Lake'. (1/4 mile)

(The 'Kirkstile Inn', be it noted, caters well for hungry and/or thirsty walkers of all tastes.)

6   Continue along this road signed as not leading to the lake and take the first turn right onto a road which is indicated as being a cul-de-sac. Within two hundred yards along this road a signposted footpath leads off to the left to the north-west corner of Crummock Water. The final stage of the path runs through an exceptionally soggy field, and in the last hundred yards of the path you will need to cross a stile crossing the wire fence which encloses this field to follow a line of tall conifer trees that leads to the water's edge. (3/4 mile)

7   Along the water's edge a path runs northwards along the top of a low concrete wall retaining the waters of the lake to its northern tip, where it crosses two footbridges spanning the lake's divided outflow. Within a hundred yards of these twin bridges a broad pathway leads northwards away from the lake back to the walk's starting point. (3/4 mile)

GRISEDALE

Distance	7 miles
Total Feet of Ascent	700 feet
Suggested Time	3 hours
Starting Point	Patterdale Village car park (NY 396 159)

Though not perfectly level this walk should be well within the range of even the most unenergetic of walkers, yet from it can be appreciated some of the wildest mountain terrain in the Lake District. Grisedale is an impressive valley. It is the largest valley of those valleys in the Lake District which do not have a surfaced road, apart from Ennerdale. The head of the valley is overlooked by some huge imposing crags. All this is possible to view and appreciate with relatively little effort, yet a few miles away in the village of Patterdale one is hardly aware of such magnificence existing at all.

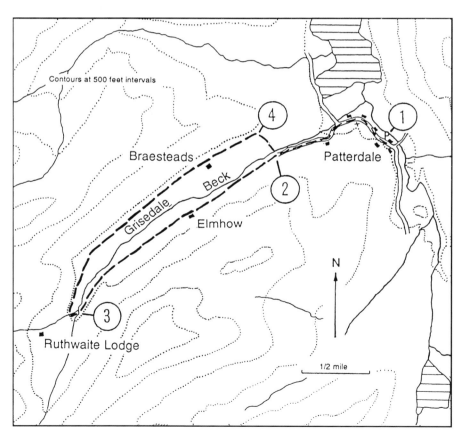

1   From Patterdale car park walk northwards along the road 700 yards past the church and take the first turn left on to a unsignposted surfaced road. This road soon splits in two. Take the right branch which soon curves right climbing uphill a hundred feet or so before levelling out. After a short distance of level walking an uninterrupted view of Grisdedale is obtained shortly after which a trackway, signposted for Helvellyn, veers off to the right. (1 mile)

2   Ignore this trackway and continue progressing forward on the surfaced roadway. After a short distance the road splits in two with the right hand branch crossing over a stone bridge and leading to Braesteads Farm. Ignore this branch and continue walking straight ahead. The road soon becomes roughly surfaced trackway. Passing Elmhow Farm it becomes rougher still and beyond an isolated barn, a couple of hundred yards further on from Elmhow, it reduces to a bridleway, which after a few hundred feet of climbing eventually comes to a wooden footbridge crossing over Grisedale Beck. (2 1/4 miles)

3   Crossing over the footbridge the bridleway continues climbing uphill roughly parallel to a tributary of Grisedale Beck flowing from Ruthwaite Cove. About two hundred yards from the Grisedale Beck footbridge is a second footbridge crossing over this tributary. Cross over this second footbridge and follow the path that leads from it back down Grisedale on the northern side of the valley. Eventually, just before reaching a wooden kissing gate, the path is crossed by a path leading down from Striding Edge. (2 1/2 miles)

4   Here turn right and follow the Striding Edge path, through a small gate in the wall to your right, downhill through another kissing gate onto a trackway that leads over a stone bridge and back to the road which you began on. Here turn left and retrace your route back to Patterdale. (1 1/4 miles)

LANGSTRATH

Distance	7 1/2 miles
Total feet of Ascent	500 feet
Suggested Time	3 hours
Starting Point	Rosthwaite Village Car Park, next to village hall
	5 miles south of Keswick (NY 258 148)

No other level walk in the Lake District affords a better insight into the wild nature of the Cumbrian Hills than this particular walk up Langstrath. The name Langstrath simply means long valley, and it is. There are no farms or houses in it, just a single ruin, the rest is wild and empty. In summer it has some popularity with bathers as there is deep pool in Langstrath Beck called Black Moss Pot, near to where the path passes through a sheep fold, which makes an excellent swimming pool.

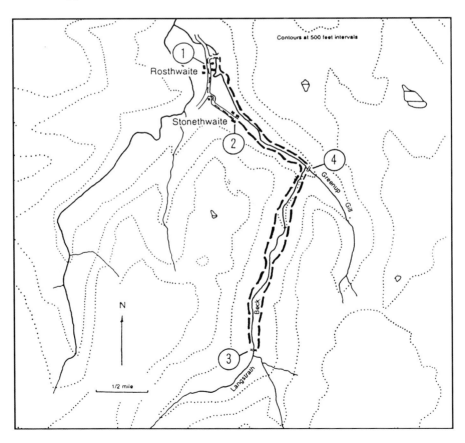

1   From Rosthwaite continue south along the main valley road and take the first turn left along the road to the hamlet of Stonethwaite. (1 mile)

2   At the end of the hamlet, just past the Langstrath Hotel, the road continues as a rough trackway initially climbing uphill slightly. Three quarters of a mile from Stonethwaite the track turns south into the valley of Langstrath. Just over a mile along the valley the trackway comes to a five bar gate. After passing through this gateway the track becomes a slightly indistinct pathway crossing a broad flat grassy section of valley floor. The path becomes more evident after a few hundred yards on reaching slightly rockier ground. Just before reaching the confluence of Stake Beck with Langstrath Beck the path comes to a sturdy footbridge spanning Langstrath Beck. (2 3/4 miles)

3   Cross over the footbridge and before climbing uphill bear left a few yards, to avoid a fairly soggy section of fellside. After climbing fifty feet of so you will come upon a distinct pathway. Here turn left and follow the path northwards along the eastern side of the valley to the confluence of Langstrath Beck and Greenup Gill. After one and three-quarter miles the path comes to a footbridge crossing over Langstrath Beck. Be sure not to cross this footbridge but continue northwards along the path another quarter of a mile to a second footbridge spanning Greenup Gill. (2 miles)

4   Cross over the footbridge and turn left and follow the pathway running along the north-eastern side of the river. This soon becomes to a broad attractive trackway leading back to Rosthwaite. On reaching a surfaced access road turn left across a stone bridge back into the centre of the village. (1 3/4 miles)

BORROWDALE

Distance	8 miles
Total feet of Ascent	1200 feet
Suggested time	4 hours
Starting Point	Keswick (NY 266 235)

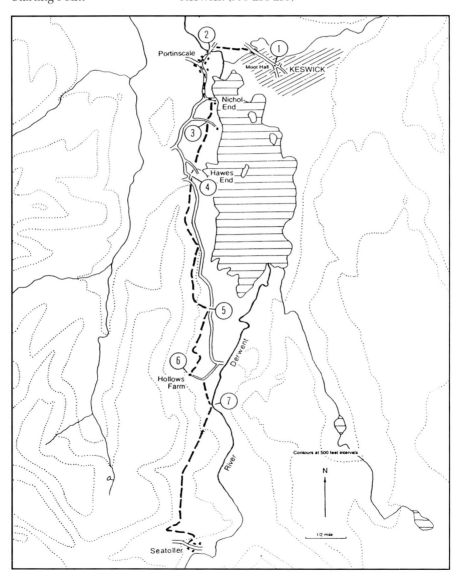

This is a terraced walk through reputedly the most beautiful valley in England. The walk depends on making the return journey by bus from Seatoller. It can also be shortened by using the lake launch to reach Hawes End. Information on these services can be obtained from the Information Centre in the Moot Hall in the centre of Keswick.

1   From the Moot Hall walk westwards downhill along Main Street to the bridge crossing the river Greta. After crossing the bridge turn immediately left onto a trackway following the river and pass through the first gate on your right. From the gate a broad path crosses two large fields to a roadway. Here turn left to reach a suspended footbridge. (1 mile)

2   Cross the bridge and continue into Portinscale village. On reaching a T junction turn left. Turn off the road when you reach a driveway leading off to the left signposted as leading to Nichol End. On reaching the lakeshore continue along a trackway to your right leading behind Nichol End Marine which cuts across a surfaced driveway and then follows the boundary fence of the garden to Fawe Park house eventually reaching another surfaced driveway. (1 1/4 miles)

3   Cross the driveway and pass through a gate giving access to a path signposted as leading to Cat Bells. The path leads to yet another driveway. Cross this driveway onto a path directly opposite which, climbing uphill slightly, within a hundred yards or so brings you to a roadway. (3/4 mile)

4   Follow this road uphill to a cattle grid. Pass through a kissing gate to the left of the grid onto a path which climbing uphill soon links onto the road again. Immediately opposite, on the other side of the road, is the start of a distinct trackway which traverses the side of the Cat Bells ridge. At one point, at the site of an old quarry, the trackway briefly rejoins the road but then immediately veers off to the right again. On reaching a stone wall the track narrows to a pathway. Passing the wall it broadens into a trackway again and leads downhill to a five bar gate a hundred yards from the roadway. (1 3/4 miles)

5   From the gate, leading off to the right, intially following a wire fence, is a pathway signposted as leading to Rosthwaite. The path, with a few undulations, roughly contours the fellside and eventually reaches a small waterworks. Here turn left and follow a wall downhill to where a trackway makes an hairpin bend. Here turn right and follow the lower section of the trackway to Hollows Farm. (1 mile)

6   Pass through the farm onto the farm access road. 200 yards from the farm an unsurfaced trackway veers off to the right leading to the river Derwent's edge where it makes a wide curve. (1/2 mile)

7   From the corner of this curve a trackway, signposted as leading to Honister, continues uphill following Broadslack Gill. After a climb of roughly 500 feet the track levels. About a hundred yards along this level section, marked with a large cairn and a blue waymark, a path branches off to the left. Follow the path which traverses the fellside above a fell wall eventually meeting the old Honister Pass toll road. Here turn left and follow the track down to Seatoller. (2 miles)

THE ROTHAY CIRCUIT

Distance	8 1/2 miles
Total feet of Ascent	500 feet
Suggested Time	3 hours
Starting Point	Ambleside Market Cross (NY 376 046)

The Rothay is the name of the river flowing from Grasmere to Ambleside, hence the name of this walk, though it could well be called the Wordsworth Walk, as it passes within a hundred yards of his grave in Grasmere in St Oswald's churchyard and also past two of his Lakeland homes; Rydal Mount, where he lived almost half his lifetime, and the more famous Dove Cottage, both of which are open to the public. There is no doubting though that if Wordsworth were alive today he would be horrified at how much Lakeland has changed, particulary this part of it where he lived for so much of his life. The modern A591 has done much to destroy the rural peace this Lakeland valley doubtless once possessed. However this walk, at least in parts, helps to recapture a sense of that more tranquil past.

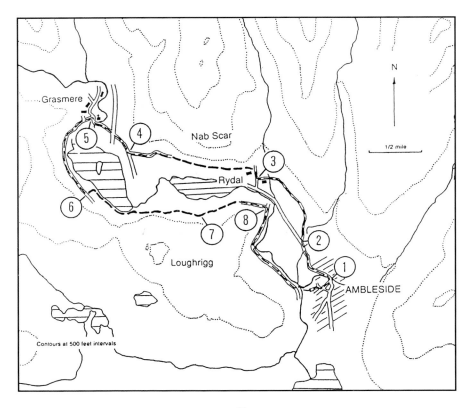

1   Follow the main road out of Ambleside northwards towards Keswick. After leaving the town and crossing over a small bridge, turn right off the road on to what looks to be a private driveway with some imposing cast-iron gates to Rydal Hall. A public footpath sign nearby however indicates that the driveway is in fact a right of way.(1/2 mile)

2   Follow the driveway through the attractive grounds of the Hall up to the Hall itself. Here the driveway runs round the back of the Hall and joins a surfaced roadway running uphill through the hamlet of Rydal. Where there might be any doubt near to the Hall as to which trackway to follow, a series of prominent footpath signs clearly indicate the correct route to take.(1 mile)

3   On reaching the road turn right. Immediately after passing Rydal Mount turn left onto an obvious trackway signposted being as a public bridleway to Grasmere. This is a very pleasant route that traverses the lower slopes of Nab Scar. Eventually, a little surprisingly, it becomes surfaced and gradually widens to become a roadway, soon after which it comes to a road junction.(1 1/2 miles)

4   Here turn right and follow the road downhill past Dove Cottage and across the main A591, where it becomes Stock Lane, into the village of Grasmere.(1/2 mile)

(There are a number tea rooms in Grasmere but in winter they virtually all close. The only exception is likely to be the cafe in the Garden Centre which hasn't so far put a ban on dogs either, at least not well-behaved ones. Whilst there are two pleasant outdoor tea places near the village green, my own preference is the small tea hut by the boat landings. It is pleasantly rickety and has a very peaceful and appealing view over the lake. It is situated a quarter of a mile from the church on the road described below in the following direction note.)

5   Walk a few yards past St Oswald's Church and turn left onto the road signposted as leading to the Information Centre. Follow the road for approximately half a mile till you locate a six bar gate on your left, over which is a fine uninterrupted view of the lake. Sited almost imperceptibly in the lefthand wall leading to the gate is a narrow gap through which is a small flight of wooden steps, and a sign indicating that it is the start of a permissive lake shore path.(1 mile)

6   Follow the path and on reaching the outflow of the lake, about forty yards before reaching the rather sturdy footbridge that crosses it, follow the small path that veers off to the right. On reaching a small crest the path splits in two. Keep to the righthand branch, the higher one, traversing along the lower slopes of Loughrigg above Rydal Water. This path reaches quite a spectacualar 'cavern', the result of past quarrying, which is well worth some exploration.(1 1/2 miles)

7   From the 'cavern' the path descends down to the left and becomes a trackway that upgrades to a surfaced roadway at a group of cottages. Within half a mile the road comes to a junction.(3/4 mile)

8   Here turn right. Follow the road for about a mile. After crossing a cattle grid on the lefthand side is a sturdy stone footbridge crossing over the river Rothay. Immediately on the other side of the bridge is the start of two paths. Both lead into Ambleside, the righthand path more directly. (1 1/2 miles)

THE CRUMMOCK WATER CIRCUIT

Distance	8 1/2 miles
Total feet of Ascent	700 feet
Suggested Time	4 hours
Starting Point	Buttermere village car park (NY 174 169)

Few people seem to walk the complete circuit of Crummock Water, certainly nowhere near the numbers that walk round Buttermere, maybe because it is thought the circuit requires too much road walking along the busy B5289. In fact it is possible to restrict such road walking to little more than half a mile. There are some striking views on the circuit, either towards Grasmoor or along the length of the lake towards the head of the Buttermere valley. There is also the possibility of visiting a pub half way round.

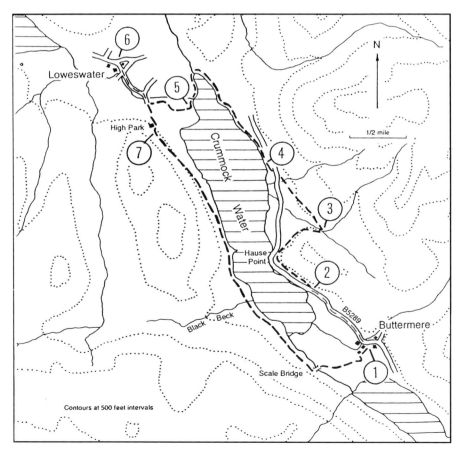

1   Starting from the village of Buttermere begin walking northwards along the B5289. Almost a hundred yards before the B5289 comes to follow the lakeshore of Crummock Water veering off to the right, indicated with a small wooden signpost, is the start of a grassy bridleway. (3/4 mile)

2   It is my guess that this humble path was once the main route into the valley before a road was forged around Hause Point, the protruding crag that juts into the lake over which the path crosses. Descending the other side of the crag the path rejoins the road. Walk fifty yards along the road and branch right onto a signposted footpath following the outer side of a boundary wall. The path soon comes to a footbridge crossing Rannerdale Beck. (1 mile)

3   Cross over the bridge and turn left to follow a path leading back towards the lake to rejoin the B5289. Continue northwards along the road a few hundred yards and pass through a kissing gate on the left-hand side of the road giving access to Fletcher Fields. From the gate a path leads down to the lakeshore of Crummock Water. (3/4 mile)

4   The path continues as a lakeshore path round the northern end of Crummock Water. The north-western part of the lake has a low concrete retaining wall. Where this wall concludes the path crosses a wooden stile which spans a wire fence. (1 1/2 miles)

5   At this point to visit the hamlet of Loweswater and the Kirkstile Inn turn right and follow the fence you have just crossed. (If however you do not wish to do this you can of course simply continue following the lakeshore path.) A few yards along the fence is a second stile. After crossing this second stile turn left. A narrow path winds through a field of soggy vegetation to a third stile. After this third stile the path is more distinct. A fourth stile and then a gate follows and the path arrives at the terminus of a surfaced road. Turn right. The road soon comes to a junction. Here turn left to reach the hamlet of Loweswater. (3/4 mile)

6   To return to the lakeshore retrace your steps to the point where you joined the roadway. Here instead of turning left onto the path you formerly followed continue straight ahead along a trackway leading past High Park Farm. As you pass the end of the garden at the back of the house look to your right. Set in the field boundary wall up to your right is a stone stile with a sign indicating that it is the start of a path to Crummock Water. (1/2 mile)

7   This path gradually descends to the lakeshore where it merges with the lakeshore path. Approaching Black Beck the path splits in two. Even though the right-hand branch crosses a footbridge it is the left-hand branch which is easiest to follow. Within a short distance this merges with a much bolder path leading down from Scale Force, and within half a mile from this point the path comes to Scale Bridge. Leading from the bridge is a broad trackway which leads back to Buttermere village. (3 1/4 miles)

THE TWO LANGDALES

Distance	8 1/2 miles
Total feet of Ascent	1000 feet
Suggested Time	4 hours
Starting Point	Elterwater (NY 328 048).
Car Parking	Car park in the centre of the village.

Because of the very nature of the Lake District there are few possible long level circular walks. This walk is about the longest there is of this type in the central Lakes, if you ignore the odd few undulations that make it less than perfectly flat. Almost the exact same circuit can be done by car, but then you would never be able to appreciate the full majesty of Great Langdale from a car as you can by walking, and indeed there are sections of this route, particularly in Little Langdale, that evoke the thought of just how wonderful the world must have been before the invention of the combustion engine.

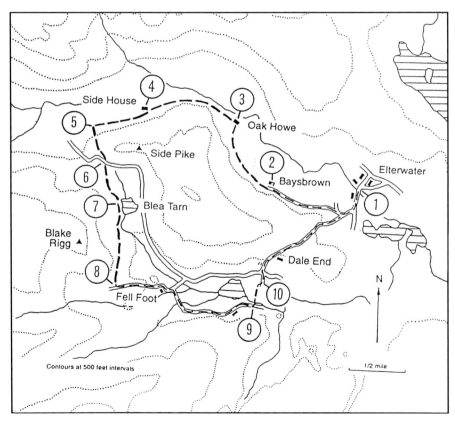

1   From the centre of the village follow the road signposted as leading to Coniston and Little Langdale. Take the first turn right. This narrow lane soon forks. Follow the righthand surfaced branch indicated as being a cul de sac to Baysbrown Farm. (1 1/4 miles)

2   On reaching the farm the lane continues straight ahead as an unsurfaced track-way. A few hundred yards along this track another trackway branches off to the right; however this is not a right of way. It is the second trackway branching off to the right, a few more yards further on after a slight climb, which you should follow. A small sign indicates that this is a right of way. This trackway reduces to a footpath leading to Oak Howe. (3/4 mile)

3   Immediately facing the barn at Oak Howe turn left onto what is initially a very grassy pathway. This is a distinct path and follows an undulating course to Side House Farm. Just before the entrance to the farm is a small footbridge. Do not cross over this bridge, but instead follow the rather faint path to the left, following the side of the beck over which the bridge crosses, uphill to a prominent wooden wall stile. (1 mile)

4   Over this stile the path continues straight ahead. However in places it is very indistinct and easy to lose. Two guiding points to look for are firstly another wall stile, and much further on, a five bar gate situated just above a group of conifer trees. From this five bar gate the path continues straight ahead to a second five bar gate in a stone wall. (3/4 mile)

5   Here the path turns left following the wall, uphill to the crest of the gap between Side Pike and Blake Rigg, to a tall wooden stile. (1/4 mile)

6   Climb over the stile and cross straight over the roadway on the other side and along the wall opposite onto a piece of cobbled pathway which continues as a distinct path leading to the small wood on the western banks of Blea Tarn. (1/2 mile)

7   Entering the copse the path splits in two. Take the lefthand lower path. Emerging from the wood the path links up with a cobbled path. Here turn right. Within a few yards the cobbled path meets a kissing gate. From here the path continues downhill by a stream initially and then veers to the right, away from the stream, to link up with the Wrynose Pass road. (3/4 mile)

8   Here turn left and follow the road downhill. Approximately a hundred yards after passing Fell Foot farm at the bottom of the hill turn right off the road over an elegant little stone bridge onto a trackway. Passing over a second bridge, next to an isolated cottage, the track curves eastwards. Where it forks take the lefthand branch towards a group of cottages. About another hundred yards past the last cottage is a kissing gate in the wall to your left. (1 1/2 miles)

9   Through this gate a path leads down to Slater's Bridge. Cross over the bridge and follow the path on the other side straight uphill to a farm access road ignoring the path branching to the right. (1/4 mile)

10 Here turn left. On reaching the road turn left and then immediately right onto another narrow lane indicated as being unsuitable for motor vehicles. Passing Dale End Farm the reason for the road's unsuitability for cars becomes evident, as here it becomes a rough unsurfaced trackway leading directly back to Elterwater. (1 1/2 miles)

WALKS LOCATION MAP

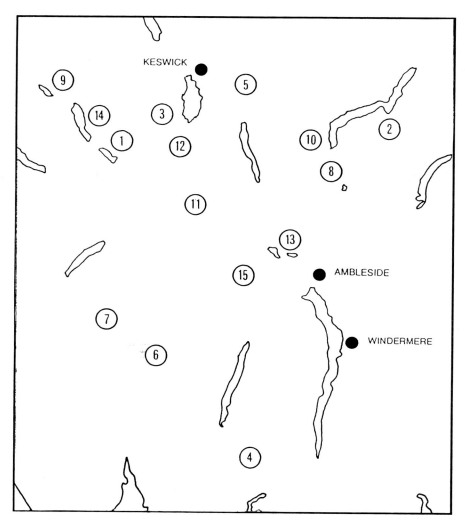